WHEN IN ROME

A Kid's Guide To Rome, Italy

PHOTOGRAPHY BY JOHN D. WEIGAND
POETRY BY PENELOPE DYAN

Bellissima Publishing, LLC
Jamul, California
www.bellissimapublishing.com

ISBN 978-1-935630-00-5

First Edition

For Kids Who Love To Travel
And For Parents Who Love
To Travel With Them!

When In Rome

Bellissima Publishing, LLC

Introduction

Rome! Magnificent Rome! From the lights of Rome at night to its busy days, there is excitement and magic in the air! There is truly no place quite like Rome. So take a walk through history as you and your child uncover the old Rome and marvel at the splendor of today's Rome. Tour the Colosseum and hear the tales of the games played there. Imagine you are a citizen of old Rome and see how exciting and modern these old Romans really were!

Enjoy the photography of John D. Weigand and the poetry of Penelope Dyan as you trace their footsteps through time and marvel at all the glory of the Vatican. Climb the Spanish steps and toss a coin in the Trevi Fountain and make a wish.

And remember as you smile and laugh with your child as they are introduced to Rome, that there is truly no place like home, unless you're in Rome; and add this book to your Bellissima travel books for kids that look simply great on your coffee table!

When In Rome

Bellissima Publishing, LLC

WHEN IN ROME
A Kid's Guide To Rome, Italy

PHOTOGRAPHY BY JOHN D. WEIGAND
POETRY BY PENELOPE DYAN

There's no place like home
unless you're in Rome.
And you can see it without fuss,
from the top of a double decker bus!

You can see a pyramid built of grey stone.
Yes, you can see it, right there in Rome!
And it reaches up so high
That it nearly touches the sky.

You can have a special treat,
of warm chestnuts cooking
right there on the street.

Below the Spanish steps there is a fountain shaped like a boat, that was never, ever meant to float.

And you can hear the most curious thing.
as the church bells atop the Spanish Steps ring!

To the colosseum you can walk when you get off the bus. . .

Or you can peddle a bicycle that looks like a car. . .

You can take, a taxi or a horse and carriage
if you think it's too far,
And you can go right next to the colosseum to the old Rome. . .

Where handsome Roman centurions and others
once lived and called home!

In the colosseum the games took place.

Down there on the stage was the starting place!

It was all within walking distance from old ancient Rome, where the Roman senators and soldiers made their home.

And the buildings were so grand with pillars tall and strong. . .

That it makes you wonder what went wrong,
and why and what happened so long past,
that ancient Rome just could not last.

You can see the Swiss Army guards at the Vatican
(a country of its own)
that existed during a part of the time
that we call ancient Rome.

And you can see Michelangelo's Pieta. . .

And beautiful paintings on Saint Peter's cathedral walls. . .

And a wondrous fountain at the Vatican lit so bright. . .
that shines in glory throughout the night.
And as you ponder it all and as you look and stare,
you know ONE thing is certain. YOU'RE in Saint Peter's Square!

You can make a wish by tossing a coin in the Trevi fountain. . .
that assures to Rome you will return,
and there are many, many other things
that you can see and learn.

And as you look at the Vatican at night. . .

You realize something about Rome just feels so right!
So learn the lessons this city has to tell.
Listen carefully and learn them well.
And never, ever make the assumption,
that a great nation can't fall from corruption.
The fact that Rome fell is no mystery,
because it is captured in the pages of Roman history.
And now the archeologists are uncovering the past,
of a once great ancient Rome that was MEANT to last.
So step back into history,
and come and see just what I see.
Because even though there is no place like home,
it is ALWAYS fun to visit Rome!

CPSIA information can be obtained
at www.ICGtesting.com
234322LV00002B